Mastering Media

Entertainment and Gaming

Stergios Botzakis

Chicago, Illinois

www.heinemannraintree.com

Visit our website to find out more information about Heinemann-Raintree books.

To order:

☎ Phone 888-454-2279

💻 Visit www.heinemannraintree.com to browse our catalog and order online.

© 2011 Raintree
an imprint of Capstone Global Library, LLC
Chicago, Illinois

Visit our website at
www.heinemannraintree.com

Edited by Adam Miller, Andrew Farrow, and Adrian Vigliano
Designed by Steve Mead
Original illustrations © Capstone Global Library Ltd.
Picture research by Elizabeth Alexander
Production by Alison Parsons
Originated by Capstone Global Library Ltd.
Printed and bound by South China Printing Company Ltd.

14 13 12 11 10
10 9 8 7 6 5 4 3 2 1

Library of Congress Cataloging-in-Publication Data
Botzakis, Stergios.
  Entertainment and Gaming / Stergios Botzakis.
     p. cm.—(Mastering media)
  Includes bibliographical references and index.
  ISBN 978-1-4109-3844-2 (hardcover)
  1. Performing arts. 2. Mass media. I. Title.
  PN1584.B68 2010
  791—dc22
2010003544

Acknowledgments
We would like to thank the following for permission to reproduce photographs: Alamy pp. 10 (© Photos 12), 13 (© DigitalDarrell), 16 (© Photos 12), 29 (© Trinity Mirror / Mirrorpix), 38 (© David Crausby); © Capstone Global Library Ltd p. 34 left; Corbis pp. 4 (© Issei Kato/Reuters), 14 (© Nintendo/ Reuters/Toru Hana), 19 (© Rune Hellestad), 24 (© Larry Marano /Retna Ltd.), 30 (© HO/Reuters), 41 (© David Brabyn), 44 (© Denis O'Regan), 47 (© Fred Prouser/Reuters); Corbis SABA p. 20 (© Najlah Feanny); Getty Images pp. 6 (Keystone Features), 9 (William Andrew), 31 (Kevork Djansezian), 36 (Doug Kanter/Bloomberg); © Guardian News and Media Limited 2010 p. 32; IGA Worldwide p. 35; Photolibrary p. 49 (John Lund/Marc Romanelli); Rex Features pp. 15 (© Warner Br/Everett), 46 (© 20thC.Fox/Everett), 48 (Nigel Howard/Evening Standard); Shutterstock p. 42 (© mostafa fawzy); The Kobal Collection pp. 22 (WARNER BROS/Sidney Baldwin), 26 top (WARNER BROS/LEGENDARY PICTURES), 26 bottom (WARNER BROS/LEGENDARY PICTURES), 34 right (Universal); TopFoto pp. 8 (J. C. TOWERS/ClassicStock), 18 (© National Pictures).

Cover photograph of Chinese visitors to "ChinaJoy", a three-day electronic games exhibition, in Shanghai, 21 July 2005, reproduced with permission of Corbis/© MING MING/Reuters.

We would like to thank Devorah Heitner for her invaluable help in the preparation of this book.

Every effort has been made to contact copyright holders of any material reproduced in this book. Any omissions will be rectified in subsequent printings if notice is given to the publisher.

Disclaimer
All the Internet addresses (URLs) given in this book were valid at the time of going to press. However, due to the dynamic nature of the Internet, some addresses may have changed, or sites may have changed or ceased to exist since publication. While the author and publisher regret any inconvenience this may cause readers, no responsibility for any such changes can be accepted by either the author or the publisher.

Contents

A World of Entertainment 4

A Short History of Entertainment Media 6

Why Create Entertainment? 10

Violence and Sex in Entertainment 16

Representations and Stereotypes 26

The Price of Entertainment 32

Stealing Entertainment 36

The Future of Entertainment Media 42

Timeline 50

Glossary *52*

Find Out More *54*

Index *56*

Some words are printed in bold, **like this**. You can find out what they mean by looking in the glossary.

A World of Entertainment

No matter what your interests and hobbies, instant entertainment is at your fingertips 24 hours a day.

Think about a typical day in your life. You probably experience a wide variety of entertainment, ranging from music to video games to television to movies. You can enjoy these different entertainment **media** no matter where you are, by using devices like MP3 players, handheld video game **consoles**, and **smartphones** (such as, iPhones and BlackBerries). In many ways, all of this entertainment adds to the quality of life. It allows people with different passions to instantly find things that inspire them.

But there is a downside as well. With entertainment so easy to access, some people find themselves spending large amounts of time sitting in front of their computers, video game consoles, televisions, or smartphones—and not interacting with the world.

As people are constantly surrounded by entertainment, they can become numb to what they are viewing. This sort of **passive** viewing can cause people to stop asking questions about the information they are receiving. This is especially a problem when some entertainment media present troubling examples of violence, sex, or unfair **stereotypes**, or when advertising tries to sell things without people noticing.

Join the entertainment revolution!

It is possible to become an active, rather than a passive, participant in the entertainment revolution. Look carefully at the various forms of entertainment you enjoy. Step back and examine the messages you are seeing, who is sending them, and why.

Once you are prepared to explore it, an incredible world of experience—and fun—is at your fingertips!

A Short History of Entertainment Media

Once television became popular, many families began to structure their evenings around popular television programs.

Until very recently, access to entertainment was very different than it is today. Two hundred years ago, people had access to few basic entertainment **media**. They could read books and newspapers, which they would have to buy from a local bookseller or newsstand. For any kind of performance, they would have to visit theaters or attractions like traveling circuses.

Recorded music

In the late 1800s, machines called gramophones and phonographs became popular. By placing large, grooved discs or cylinders on these machines, people could play recorded music. These machines became known as record players. Later technological innovations included cassette tapes (beginning in the 1960s), compact discs or CDs (beginning in the 1980s), and **MP3s** (electronic files used to store songs, beginning in the 1990s).

The rise of movies

In the 1890s, movies became a new entertainment medium. The first films were in black and white, with no sound. By the late 1920s, sound became a part of movies, and color was perfected in the 1930s. Movie stars and movies quickly became hugely popular all around the world.

Radio enters people's homes

The next major entertainment media was radio. Beginning in the 1920s, radio stations broadcasted music, sports, and news, as well as comedies, dramas, and variety shows.

The revolution of television

Television was developed in the 1930s, but it was not in many people's homes until the late 1940s and the 1950s. Television took many popular programs from radio, such as soap operas and adventure shows. From early in its history, however, some people worried that television distracted people from other things, such as reading, spending time with friends, or getting exercise.

Ever-changing technology

If early television viewers were busy during a particular broadcast or simply forgot to tune in, that was it—they lost their chance to see it. This changed in the 1970s, as recording devices like videocassette recorders (VCRs) came into use. People could use videocassettes to tape programs and watch them at a later date.

VCRs and videotapes also allowed people to buy and rent copies of movies and other programming. This opened a whole new entertainment world. Starting in the 1990s, the rise of **digital** versatile disk (DVD) players, **digital video recorders (DVRs)** like TiVo, and Blu-ray players continued the possibilities of recorded entertainment.

Arcade games like *Ms. Pac-Man* were very popular in the 1970s and 1980s.

In the early days of television, viewers had just a handful of stations to choose from. This changed with the rise of cable television in the early 1980s. Suddenly, for an extra fee, people could get dozens—and later hundreds—of different channels, often 24 hours a day.

In the 1970s and 1980s, video arcades became popular with many people. By putting a coin in the slot, people could play games like *Pac-Man* and *Donkey Kong*. Around the same time, companies like Atari and Nintendo began creating video game **consoles** that people could hook up to their televisions to play similar games at home.

Since the 1990s, digital effects and sound have made it possible to create video games that would have been impossible to experience in the past. Using consoles like the X-Box, PlayStation, or Wii, or personal computers, players can have experiences ranging from silly fun to a very realistic simulation of flying an airplane or fighting in a war.

During the 1970s and 1980s, personal computers became affordable enough for most people to have them in their homes. In the 1990s, the Internet developed dramatically, allowing people to share information, images, and video like never before.

For all these entertainment media, technology is still changing all the time. For example, effects such as **computer-generated imagery (CGI)** in movies like *Transformers* (2007) and *Avatar* (2009) would have been unimaginable to filmmakers even in the 1990s. And the development of MP3 files has changed the way people buy and listen to music.

Technology is also becoming increasingly portable, as people can use a tiny **smartphone** to listen to MP3s, watch a movie, or look at a website, no matter where they are.

Did you know?

Video games have overtaken movies as the most popular form of entertainment media. The video game *Halo 3* made $170 million on the day it was released. The single-day record for a movie debut is $72.7 million, for 2009's *The Twilight Saga: New Moon.*

Wireless and smartphone technologies have had huge impacts on our everyday lives.

Why Create Entertainment?

Movies like *Transformers: Revenge of the Fallen* make movie studios lots of money and give moviegoers a fun experience.

So, people have created various kinds of entertainment throughout history. But why?

One reason is personal expression. People create works of art—whether they are musicians, filmmakers, or any other kind of artist—to express an emotion or idea. In many cases, they create art so they can share these emotions and ideas with other people.

Entertainment is also fun, pure and simple. People who create silly humor or exciting video games want to have fun themselves and share it with the world.

Of course, entertainment offers opportunities to make money. Entertainment **industries** that make movies, television programs, video games, and music make billions of dollars a year, which is more than the budgets of some small countries! Creating successful movies, video games, and so on is therefore very serious business for people working in these industries. They must focus on finding the perfect formula for success.

Reasons to entertain

Most entertainment **media** today are created for a blend of these reasons. For example, a musician may have a passion for music and expression, while her **record label** (a company that makes music recordings) has plans to make millions of dollars off of her music. Or a silly movie that provides people with laughs is also a way for a movie studio (company that makes movies) to create a major hit starring an internationally famous actor.

People enjoy different works of art for different reasons. But the next time you enjoy a work of entertainment, ask yourself: Why was this made in the first place? Why were certain choices made?

Finding out what you like

When it comes to big-budget entertainment, major companies do not take many chances. For example, a single action film can cost $200 million, so major movie studios do their research before making an action movie.

Market research is what many entertainment companies do in order to determine what they will make. This involves a group of studies done to figure out what **consumers** (people who buy things) want, need, or believe.

Focusing on an audience

Once they have a product, a company shows it to **focus groups**. These are small groups of people who are asked to give their opinions. These people represent the type of people the product will appeal to. Another name for an intended audience is the **target demographic**.

Watching trends

Another common activity in market research is trend watching. Entertainment companies figure out what is popular and then try to make more of the same. An example of such a trend is the *Twilight* books by U.S. author Stephenie Meyer. After the huge success of the books and movies based on them, the vampire theme was used in a number of new books, television shows, video games, and movies.

Companies that create entertainment media know how valuable it is for their media to appeal to teens.

Teenagers have some of the most disposable income (money they can spend how they want) of any group of people. They do not generally have bills to pay, so their money can go toward entertainment. As a result, teens are the target demographic for many entertainment media. Their likes and dislikes will often inspire what gets made.

Movie studios will sometimes change a movie based on what test audiences tell them.

Testing

For many products, the next step is testing. Video game manufacturers ask experienced video game players to test new games. These testers' job is to find the glitches and parts of the game that are too easy or difficult, or not exciting enough.

Moviemakers usually pick test audiences based on a certain target demographic. For example, if moviemakers want to see how teenagers like an action movie, they get a theater full of teens. The audience members get to see the movie for free. When it ends, they give feedback.

Did you know?
Entertainment media make a lot of money. In 2007, video games made about $40 billion worldwide. The U.S. movie industry made about $10 billion. Album sales, including **MP3** downloads, made $428 million in 2008.

Testing versus taking risks

Sometimes research and testing lead to the best possible product for the consumer. For example, a movie that does not tell a clear story will benefit from audience feedback. Similarly, by using research into what people wanted, Nintendo invented the successful Wii (see box below).

Market research in action: The Wii

The Nintendo Wii was designed in response to issues that came up in market research. People became annoyed by the big tangle of wires coming from their game systems. So, Nintendo made the Wii wireless. Some people complained of the high prices of video game systems and their large sizes. So, Nintendo made the unit as inexpensive and small as possible.

Nintendo was taking a big risk by introducing a new product. Since a failure would cost the company a lot of money, it tested the Wii with company employees and their family members.

Soon after the Wii was released, some people found the straps that connected the controllers to their hands broke too easily. People were accidentally throwing their controllers at their televisions! But with this exception, due to good research and testing, the Wii became a huge success for Nintendo. In 2009 the Wii beat competing **consoles** PlayStation 3 and Xbox 360 in worldwide sales.

Sometimes when entertainment companies create something based solely on research, it falls flat. Have you ever seen an action movie sequel that lacked any of the fun of the original? Or heard a copycat pop band whose songs were utterly forgettable? That is the danger of having money rather than creative ideas drive the creation of entertainment.

However, entertainment media are learning that audiences sometimes want something creative and new, rather than something made based on studies and tests. This was proven in 2009 with the success of the movie *Where the Wild Things Are* (see box at right).

Think about the entertainment you like best. Why do you think it was made in the first place?

Beyond market research: Creative vision

U.S. movie director Spike Jonze is known for creating strange, imaginative music videos and movies. He was asked to bring his imagination to a movie version of the popular children's book *Where the Wild Things Are*. When movie studio executives were shown test screenings of the movie, it was unlike anything they had seen before. However, some of them said it was too strange and too scary for children and so the studio pushed for Jonze to change it. They had put a lot of money into the film and wanted to see a **profit** (earn money). But Jonze held firm that the movie was the way he meant it to be and should not be changed.

In the end, Jonze won out—and the movie surprised many people by being a big box office success in 2009. This made movie studios rethink their strict reliance on testing and safe choices.

The movie *Where the Wild Things Are* featured amazing, and strange, costumes and locations.

Violence and Sex in Entertainment

Audiences had mixed reactions to the violence in *Saving Private Ryan*.

With so much competition out there, people who create entertainment need to somehow stand out and get **consumers'** attention. One of the most common ways different entertainment **media** shock is by showing extreme examples of violence, and shocking or provocative images.

Is there a point?

Sometimes works of entertainment use violence to make an important point. For example, some war movies show **graphic** (realistic and detailed) images of blood and death. The first half hour of *Saving Private Ryan* (1998), a World War II film, shows a violent series of events that are confusing, brutal, and horrific.

Director Steven Spielberg argued that he used violence in the film to explore larger ideas. He said, "I would be doing an extreme disservice to veterans if this was simply one more movie that glamorized World War II." Spielberg meant to show what real soldiers went through to win the war. He hoped that audiences would see wartime sacrifices and respect soldiers for making these sacrifices. Spielberg also hoped audiences would see that decisions to go to war should not be taken lightly.

Similarly, some musicians use violent lyrics. Some rappers, for example, have argued that they are reflecting the reality of life in tough parts of the inner city, where violence is a real problem. They say their lyrics shed light on the need to address these problems.

But some critics argue that creators of violent entertainment do not always have a reason for the violence beyond shock value. This gets the attention of an audience and—if something is really shocking—it also gets reported in the news. This kind of attention brings more business and sells more tickets, **MP3s**, or video games.

Today, audiences are so used to seeing violence in entertainment that they often do not give it much thought. However, as we will see in this chapter, there is sometimes a cost to using mindless violence. You will have to ask yourself if you think the costs are worth whatever entertainment value the violence provides.

> **❝** I'm telling you there are children who are affected by those images, where those images take root and bear bitter fruit and change them, and desensitize them to the consequences of violence and make them more likely to commit it themselves. **❞**
>
> —former U.S. Vice President Al Gore

🖼 *Grand Theft Auto 4* is often criticized for its extreme violence.

Video game violence

Video games, in particular, are often criticized for their excessive violence. Of particular concern are games made to seem like real experience. In first-person shooting games, people take the point of view of a gunman and walk around shooting things. Games like the *Call of Duty* series are intended to create realistic war experiences, including shooting people.

One of the most **controversial** video games is *Grand Theft Auto 4*. In it, players have gang wars and kill whoever gets in their way, including police.

Violent movies and music

Many movies also contain a lot of violence. Popular movies like the *Terminator*, *Saw*, and *Hostel* series are full of blood and death. Some directors like Quentin Tarantino (*Kill Bill: Vol. 1, 2003*) and Guy Ritchie (*Revolver*, 2005) have made a name for themselves with films featuring high levels of graphic violence. Some people argue that these movies are meant to be over the top, and that the violence should not be taken seriously. Others argue that they send a dangerous message.

In addition to some rappers, Marilyn Manson, Slipknot, and various other bands are often criticized for the violence in their work. These bands' themes often include death, hatred, and aggression. While the artists suggest that

they are exploring characters and using their free speech, critics argue they are setting off aggression and violence in young fans.

Studies have shown that people who constantly absorb violent entertainment become numb to the violence they see. Critics of entertainment media fear that this makes some people lose their sensitivity toward horrible actions. This is called becoming **desensitized**. Some researchers worry this could cause a lack of caring about other people and the realities of human suffering. They argue that desensitized people will no longer be affected or care about the real violence that exists in the world.

Some critics have accused Marilyn Manson of causing aggression in his fans.

In real life...
The next time you see entertainment that seems violent, step back and think about what would happen if this were real life. What if you knew the person who was hurt? Who else would suffer as a result of the actions? What penalties would the people causing the violence face? These issues are often left unexamined in entertainment media.

" Just because a film has a murder scene doesn't mean people are going to commit the act... That overstates the power of the image and underestimates the role of parents. **"**

—Serge Tisseron, psychiatrist

19

Columbine

In rare cases, people who are desensitized to violence may find the line between reality and fantasy blurred.

One of the best-known examples of this happened near Denver, Colorado, in 1999. Two high school students thought up an elaborate, violent plan. The boys showed up at their high school on April 20 armed with assault weapons. They killed 13 people and wounded 24 others—and also intended to set off bombs, which failed to ignite. The people they shot were randomly chosen.

Representations of violence in the media often ignore the real-life consequences, such as the suffering felt by the students and families affected by the Columbine tragedy.

Why did it happen?

After this tragedy, people struggled to understand why it had happened. Some noted how the acts showed an incredible lack of feeling for other people. But how had the shooters become this way? Some people noted psychological problems and possible reactions to medications they were taking. Others pointed to the fact that they were bullied and treated as outsiders at school.

But others tried to focus the discussion on media, noting that the boys were obsessed with first-person shooter games like *Doom*. It was also widely reported that both were fans of Marilyn Manson, though this claim was later proved to be false.

Blaming video games

The families of the people killed filed a lawsuit against many companies who make violent video games. They argued that the games encouraged the two teens to kill others. But a judge ruled that it would take more than video games to cause such an act, and the lawsuit was dismissed. People continue to debate how much these entertainment media were to blame for this horrible tragedy.

The need to communicate

In the film *Bowling for Columbine* (2002), which examined gun violence, filmmaker Michael Moore asked singer Marilyn Manson what he would have said to the Columbine shooters (who killed themselves the day of the massacre). Manson said, "I wouldn't say a single word to them. I would listen to what they have to say, and that's what no one did."

Manson was touching on a common problem with desensitization. When young people become too absorbed in fantasy worlds of entertainment, they lose their grip on reality. Human contact and connections are needed to pull people back into the real world. Talking through feelings of violence and aggression—and being heard—can sometimes prevent things from going too far.

Real-life effects

Even if you think you are not affected, once you hear about the effects violence in entertainment media possibly have on other people, how do you feel about it? Do you think there should be limits? Or, is it possible media is just an easy target and other problems in society are more at fault?

Natural Born Killers and freedom of speech

U.S. director Oliver Stone's 1994 movie *Natural Born Killers* is a very violent and controversial film. It tells the story of a young couple in love who go on a murderous spree, eventually killing 52 people. Along the way, they become celebrities.

Some critics felt *Natural Born Killers* glamorized violence and murder. Others saw it as an artistic comment on modern entertainment and media culture.

The filmmakers said it was meant to expose how violent and obsessed with fame people had become. But many critics argued that the film made the killing spree seem glamorous and even romantic. Critics were also concerned that the couple breaks out of prison and leads a happy life together in the end, not suffering any consequences.

Copycat crimes

The movie became even more controversial when a series of "copycat" crimes began to happen. Most famous was the case of a young couple from Oklahoma who watched the movie before beginning a crime spree of their own, killing one man and then shooting and paralyzing a convenience-store clerk from the neck down.

In March 1996 the paralyzed woman and her family filed a lawsuit against Stone and the makers of the film, as well as the shooters. A supporter of the lawsuit said the movie was "designed to shock us and to further numb us to the senselessness of reckless murder. . . Oliver Stone is saying that murder is cool and fun; murder is a high, a rush. . . You will not be punished."

Free speech

In his defense, Stone said that he was using his right to free speech. In the United States, people are entitled to the right to express themselves—to have free speech—under the First Amendment to the Constitution. He meant for his movie to get people thinking about violence in society, and he felt it was his creative right to make that point however he wanted.

Stone also said, "It's not a film's responsibility to tell you what the law is. And if you kill somebody, you've broken the law." In his defense, people also argued that the real-life couple was abusing LSD, a drug that causes people to lose their grasp on reality, and also suffered from mental illness. The movie alone did not cause their actions.

When the case first came before a judge, the judge ruled that Stone was protected by the First Amendment. However the lawsuit did not end for several years. Finally, in 2001, a judge ruled that Stone was not responsible for the actions of the couple. What do you think?

Sex and entertainment media

Another surefire way for entertainment media to get attention is to show sexual images. Sexual suggestion occurs often in entertainment media, from skimpily dressed pop stars to controversial scenes on television shows. As with violence, many people are so used to constantly seeing sexual images that they do not think much about it.

Making a point

Artists argue that there is a place for sex and sexuality in entertainment. Sexuality is a healthy part of life, and when presented in the right way—in films and music intended for adults—it can be a valuable part of stories about adult relationships.

Recording artists like Rihanna often use sexuality as part of their public image.

How much is too much?

But many people worry that too many sexual messages are targeted at young people. They worry that this could cause young people to have unrealistic ideas about sex and to experiment with it before they are ready. Other people worry that such imagery presents women as "sex objects" (see pages 28 and 29).

When you see sexual images in entertainment media, ask yourself what purpose it serves. Does it tell an important story? Or is it just there to cause controversy and sell products?

Ratings systems and freedom of speech

Many governments use ratings systems to offer general guidelines about the content of entertainment. For example, the Motion Picture Association of America issues ratings for movies, ranging from G (general audiences) to NC-17 (no one under 17 will be admitted). For video games, the Entertainment Software Rating Board lists the age appropriateness of a video game, as well as why it earned that rating—for example, for violent content. CDs with potentially offensive material are given a "Parental Advisory" label.

Enforcement

Some ratings systems can be enforced by entertainment distributors. For example, a movie theater can prevent someone under 17 from entering an NC-17 movie. But ratings systems mostly leave it up to parents to decide what their kids can see and do. Many people think it is good to have these options.

Television is a bit different. All televisions within the United States are required to have V-chip technology. This means they have special receivers that can block programs the government decides are inappropriate for children. Still, it is up to parents to activate a V-chip.

Criticism

Many people complain that these ratings systems block free speech. Stores like Wal-Mart will not carry albums with "Parental Advisory" stickers and ask the artists to create "clean" versions of their albums. Critics feel this interference in artists' creations violates their right to express themselves freely.

Similarly, V-chips may prevent people from seeing a program and deciding for themselves if it is offensive. This, too, prevents free expression for the people who made the program.

What do you think is the best approach?

Representations and Stereotypes

The 2006 movie *300* was criticized for its portrayals of "good" Spartan characters and "bad" Persian characters. Some people found the portrayals in the film to be inaccurate, stereotypical, and offensive. What do you think?

With so many entertainment options out there, the people who create entertainment want to win over **consumers**. As we have seen, easy ways to do this include giving people what they want and shocking them.

Creators of different entertainment **media** sometimes also assume people want what is familiar. This can cause them to rely on using easy **stereotypes**. Stereotypes are generalizations about people as a group—for example, about a certain racial or ethnic group.

Sometimes basic stereotypes are used to tell a story quickly. For example, when you see a handsome, tall man suddenly walk in on a crime scene, he is usually the good guy. Viewers can often assume that a handsome person is a hero. Villains are usually ugly or scarred. (Examine the posters on the left for examples of these "hero and villain" stereotypes.) Stereotypes like these go back to the earliest forms of entertainment.

The dangers of stereotypes

There are many problems with relying on stereotypes. They lump people together as a group, rather than looking at people as individuals. They can also give wrong and unfair impressions of people.

Given how much people are exposed to entertainment media, the danger is that people may start to see stereotypes as fact. Rather than seeing the people they encounter in real life as individuals, they might assume that these people will act like the stereotypes presented in entertainment.

Look more closely

When looking at entertainment media, think about how various kinds of people are represented. Does it match up to the real people you know? Also, think about who is *not* shown. Just as negative stereotypes can be damaging, so can a tendency to represent a world that is free of different kinds of people. This can make these people feel they do not have a place in the world.

Women in entertainment media

Think about the women you see in various entertainment media. Chances are that many of the women who came to mind are beautiful and young. Arguably, young, beautiful women are most likely to succeed in entertainment media, whether it is television stars, movie stars, pop stars, or video game characters. Talent alone is often not enough to succeed.

A common stereotype among the portrayals in women in entertainment media is that they are **passive**. This means they rely on other people to take care of them—for example, they wait to be rescued by a hero.

Another troubling stereotype in entertainment media is that women are sometimes portrayed as "sexual objects," rather than complex human beings. For example, *Grand Theft Auto 4* has been criticized because many women in the game are presented as strippers and prostitutes—and players can choose to kill or abuse them.

> ❝ A stereotyped, sexist, and often degrading image of women is presented by the new electronic media. . . The majority of video games constitute one more element in the reproduction of discriminatory stereotypes against women. ❞
>
> —Eva-Britt Svensson, European Parliament's Women's Rights and Gender Equality Committee

Accepting stereotypes

Just as people can become used to violence, they can also become used to these sorts of representations of women. The danger is that people, especially young men, will not properly respect women if they spend lots of time watching entertainment that portrays women in a negative light.

Similarly, young women might come to think that these stereotypes are "normal" and feel that they have to follow them—focusing only on appearance, or acting overly passive or sexy—to fit in.

Role models

There are also positive role models in entertainment media. Musicians like Alicia Keys present strong, confident images. They rely on selling their talent, rather than on selling themselves as stereotypes.

In television shows like *Buffy the Vampire Slayer* and *Alias*, female lead characters defend themselves as well as other people, and they are presented as smart and complex. Television shows and movies featuring strong women as police officers, doctors, and lawyers also present women in a more complex, realistic light.

Video games may be further behind other entertainment media when it comes to moving beyond female stereotypes. In video games, women are hardly represented at all, and when they are represented it can take the form of *Grand Theft Auto 4*. Some video game characters such as Lara Croft (from the *Tomb Raider* series) are confident, capable, and able to defend themselves. However, the physical aspects of a character like Lara Croft, such as body-type and clothing, are arguably designed to make her more sexually appealing.

How do you think people's perceptions of women would be changed if there were more smart, powerful women represented in entertainment media?

Alicia Keys is known more for her music than for relying on a sexualized image.

Did you know?
About half of the people in the world are women. And about 40 percent of the people who play video games are female. But according to research, only 1 in 10 game characters is female.

Race and ethnicity

The same concerns apply to stereotypical representations of different races and ethnicities in entertainment. For example, if people only listened to entertainment media, they might think that all young black men are either star athletes or in gangs, or that all Asian people are either great students or know karate. Similarly, they could think all Italian people are connected to the Mafia.

Of course, in real life people from different races and ethnicities display a huge amount of variation from person to person. Racial and ethnic stereotypes do not show a truthful image. Stereotypes may tell us a story quickly or get an easy laugh, but they are wrong.

The dangers of stereotypes

Just as it is dangerous to present women in a certain way in entertainment media, it is also dangerous to present different races and ethnicities this way. People who have little contact with individuals outside their own group might base their understanding on image, not reality. And people from the races depicted might feel there are no opportunities in society for them to be anything beyond these stereotypes.

Think about your friends and the people you know from different backgrounds. Do they fit into stereotypes? How are they different?

Seeing critically

Pay attention to some of your favorite entertainment media and see how often you can spot racial or ethnic stereotypes. How often do you see representations that show the more complex reality of different kinds of people? Become a critical viewer!

The *Princess and the Frog* presented a new role model for black girls.

Being included

While it is painful for people to see others like themselves represented unfairly, it is also painful to not be represented at all.

The importance of being represented became apparent in reactions to the 2009 Disney animated movie *The Princess and the Frog*. For the first time in Disney history, the heroine, Tiana, was a black woman. The African American writer of the movie, Rob Edwards, expressed the importance of the movie, saying, "For so many of my friends, they've been waiting for this their whole lives." Many mothers of black daughters expressed similar enthusiasm that their daughters could see a fantasy ideal of the same ethnicity.

Pursuing diversity

Entertainment media have been moving toward presenting positive role models from different races and ethnicities. There are an increasing number of television, movie, and music stars from different backgrounds.

For example, African American actor Will Smith is the number-one movie star in the world. Colombian singer Shakira is internationally successful. And the movie *Slumdog Millionaire* (2008) made international stars of British-Indian actor Dev Patel and Indian actress Freida Pinto. All these performers play a wide variety of characters that do not rely on easy stereotypes.

Freida Pinto and Dev Patel have earned worldwide fame.

The Price of Entertainment

Internet advertising has become a major annoyance for many Internet users.

People today are used to a constant flow of entertainment, much of it free. It is easy to forget that the people who create different forms of entertainment often spend a lot of money creating their work. The creators of entertainment **media** need to make back this money—and hopefully a **profit** as well.

Some entertainment media make money by selling their products— for example, the price of a movie ticket, a new video game, or an **MP3**. But other forms of entertainment media, like television and the Internet, are basically free, except for the cost of signing up for cable and Internet connections. These media make money through advertising. On television, **networks** (companies that own channels) show commercials. On the Internet, web pages are covered in ads. In all these cases, advertisers pay the entertainment company a fee to advertise their products. This money, in turn, helps the company afford to create new entertainment.

Skipping commercials

But as technology is changing, **consumers** are finding ways to avoid looking at advertising. In recent years, television recording technology like **DVRs** has allowed people to record programming much more easily than ever before. But pre-recorded programming also gives people the ability to skip commercials altogether.

Many entertainment-related websites, such as YouTube or websites where people meet to discuss media, are free. Yet, depending on how elaborate the website is, the website creators have costs for employees, computer software, and more. To pay for these things, websites feature advertisements.

However, many consumers find Internet advertisements very annoying. As a result, "ad-blocking" programs like Adblock are being developed. These kinds of software allow people to freely view websites without ads taking over the screen.

Product placement

Advertisers are always looking for ways to reach consumers. One increasingly successful advertising strategy is called **product placement**. Companies pay entertainment media big money to put their products in movies, music videos, and video games. But unlike commercials, which consumers know are ads, product placement simply shows a product in the background of a scene.

For example, in 1982 the alien in the blockbuster movie *E.T.: The Extra-Terrestrial* was shown eating Reese's Pieces candy. Within weeks, sales of the candy went through the roof. Ever since then, movies and television shows have become full of clever examples of product placement, whether it is a Verizon phone in *Gossip Girl* or General Motors cars in *Transformers*.

Did you know?
The 2002 James Bond film *Die Another Day* made $70 million in product placement alone.

Prominent placement of the candy Reese's Pieces in *E.T.* caused a huge spike in sales of the product.

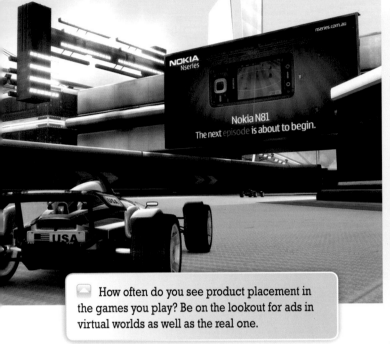

Nokia N81
The next episode is about to begin.

How often do you see product placement in the games you play? Be on the lookout for ads in virtual worlds as well as the real one.

Video games have also become a popular place for advertising. For example, if you play the *Sims* games, you can visit a Starbucks or McDonald's.

All these advertisers hope that consumers unknowingly become comfortable and familiar with their brands as a result of this placement. They also hope that by seeing their favorite stars or characters use a certain brand, people will find the brand more desirable.

Keep your eyes open

As with issues like violence and **stereotypes** in entertainment, many people **passively** accept the advertising messages that they see. But you can take charge by learning to spot product placement (see box at right). It is up to you to decide if you like the products you see and want them for yourself.

Spotting product placement

The next time you watch a movie or television show or play a video game, pay attention to the backgrounds and the products that characters use. You will see lots of advertising, even when there are no commercials. Here are some signs to look out for:

- Characters openly refer to certain brand names—for example, they might talk about shopping at a particular store or eating at a chain restaurant.
- More than one character is shown using a certain brand—for example, drinking a certain brand of soda or using a certain brand of computer.
- Camera angles focus on products—for example, a billboard advertisement or a logo in a store window is focused on, perhaps behind a character's head as he or she talks.

All these signs suggest that a company paid the creators of the entertainment media to have their products shown.

Stealing Entertainment

People sell pirated copies of popular movies in markets and on street corners throughout the world.

In recent years, **consumers** have come to expect entertainment whenever they want it. Sometimes this sense of a "right" to entertainment extends to what is in fact stealing entertainment. Now, technological changes have made it easier for people to steal, copy, and share entertainment **media** than ever before.

Pirating methods

Piracy is when people illegally copy, use, share, or sell a product such as a DVD, video game, CD, or **MP3**. People make money by selling pirated entertainment on the Internet and sometimes on city streets.

These are some of the ways that people pirate media:

Peer-to-peer sharing

Some Internet pirates crack the code that protects media files in purchased copies of DVDs, CDs, and video game discs. Then they post these files online for others to download for free. Many of these users do not make any money on this act. They do it for the challenge and to share files with other people.

"Cracked" files

Other people similarly crack these codes, but they sell their copies for a **profit**. They can make many copies for pennies and then sell those copies at a price that is a deep discount compared to what people would spend in a store.

"Modding"

Some people have figured out how to disable the codes protecting software in video game consoles. They load these **consoles** up with illegally acquired games or media files and then sell them.

Filming in a movie theater

Perhaps the simplest form of piracy is when people take video cameras into movie theaters and record new movies as they watch them. People then buy copies of the movie and avoid having to pay to see it in the theater at full price.

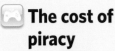

The cost of piracy

Every year, pirating costs various entertainment **industries** a lot of money:

- In 2008 the movie industry estimated that it lost over $1 billion in the United States and United Kingdom alone to piracy.
- U.S. video game companies estimate they lose at least $3.5 billion every year to piracy.
- The music industry estimates it loses $12.5 billion a year globally to piracy.

The quality of pirated movies can be terrible, as seen in this pixelated still from a pirated dvd.

Stealing from the rich

Some people argue that the companies making major entertainment media—such as movie studios, **record labels**, and video game manufacturers—are already making billions of dollars. And the artists who act in the movies or create the music are making millions of dollars themselves. Some people therefore think it is okay to not give these people any more profits.

Organized crime

However, the story is not so simple. Given the potential profits of pirating, organized crime is increasingly becoming involved in piracy. Just as they manage the sale of drugs and other illegal products, gangs and terrorist organizations are now selling pirated entertainment. So, when you save money by buying a pirated product, that money is not going into the hands of wealthy entertainment companies—but it is possibly going into the hands of criminals and terrorists.

Intellectual property

More importantly, pirating is simply illegal. When someone creates something—whether it is a song, a movie, or a video game—the law says it is that person's "intellectual property." The person owns the **copyright** to the work, meaning he or she controls how and where the work is used and has the right to benefit from any profit received from the work.

Think about it in terms of yourself. If you wrote an amazing song, but found that other people were selling a recording of it and making a profit from it, how would you feel?

Consequences

Given all the money entertainment media stand to lose to piracy, they are fighting back. For example, in 2009 entertainment industries such as the movie industry sued the Swedish makers of a website called Pirate Bay. The website did not contain pirated products, but rather directed users to where they could locate pirated material on the Internet. A court found each of the men behind Pirate Bay guilty, with each sentenced to a year in prison and given a fine of about $3.6 million.

Individuals have been pursued as well. In 2009 a Minnesota woman was fined $1.9 million for sharing 24 copyrighted songs online.

> **" I always thought that 'piracy' connotes something glamorous. Let's call it what it is: theft. I think it's just like shoplifting. "**
>
> —Barry M. Meyer, chairman and CEO, Warner Bros. Entertainment

39

Should we give it all away?

Piracy is a big problem in the entertainment media industries, but some people have a solution. They say artists should give some things away for free. If something is free, it cannot be stolen. This is an interesting strategy that seems to work well for some music and game makers.

One way that some musicians share their music is through social-networking sites. MySpace is an especially active site for this activity. Bands can make their own pages and gather fans (see page 44). They can also give people access to songs they can listen to for free.

Many bands find that people listen to the songs, and if they like them they tell their friends about the music. Once a band has a following, some people will eventually not just use the free files. Some of the new fans will buy the music.

The business model of giving people something free to make money later also seems to work for video games. *Runescape* is a free video game made by Jagex, a games company based in the United Kingdom. *Runescape* is a fantasy game in which players can create a character, go on quests, do tasks, and fight other characters. It is free to anyone to download and join. Jagex has made partnerships with advertisers to offset the costs of the free accounts.

Runescape offers more game features to people who pay for their accounts. Many players get hooked on the free version, but end up paying to get more features.

Pay what you want

In 2007, the UK band Radiohead tried a different approach to giving something away for free. They released their album *In Rainbows* online for free, saying that payment was voluntary. People could choose to download the album for free, or pay any amount they wanted for it. The band was tired of having their new albums leaked online by pirates, so they joked that they would leak it themselves.

In Rainbows remained a free download for three months. In the end, Radiohead sold more than three million copies. Radiohead's lead singer, Thom Yorke, said in an interview that the band made more money on *In Rainbows* than on all of their other albums combined. Since then many other artists, including Trent Reznor of the band Nine Inch Nails, have offered their music in this way.

Radiohead's experiment showed that giving content away for free can end up being a smart business move.

NO REALLY. IT'S UP TO YOU

HOME   VIEW BASKET

The Future of Entertainment Media

There seem to be new examples of entertainment—and new ways to explore it—every day.

Valid concerns?

Some people are worried about the rapid growth of entertainment **media**. They worry that people, especially young people, will spend enormous amounts of time in front of their televisions, video game **consoles**, or computers. All of this is at the expense of other ways people could be spending their time, such as interacting with other people, being outdoors, or doing physical activity.

People also worry about the human tendency to watch or listen to whatever is on, rather than stopping to think whether or not it is worthwhile. Some critics have suggested that some current television programs, such as shows that follow celebrities' daily lives, are "disposable" and not worth anyone's time.

A bright future

While these are valid concerns, there is also a lot to be excited about. New technologies are creating new forms of entertainment (and new ways to experience them) that people could not have dreamed of 20 years ago.

Another exciting development in entertainment is the interconnectedness provided by the Internet. Given how many websites there are to visit on the Internet, people can thoroughly explore a passion—whether it is movies, video games, or hip-hop music—and find other people who share the same interest.

Many young people are choosing to become active participants in the world of entertainment media.

Getting a big break

In the recent past, most musicians only launched their careers and got noticed by the public if they signed a deal with a major **record label**. Recent advances in entertainment media have changed all that. Thanks to social-networking sites like MySpace and video-sharing sites like YouTube, many artists can now control their own destinies.

> " I think it's a great thing, MySpace, and never mind that it benefits bands—we know that already. It opens up a lot of doors for people that want to listen to music. "
>
> —Lily Allen

Lily Allen has been savvy in her use of new entertainment media such as MySpace.

For example, in 2005, when she was 20 years old, UK singer Lily Allen began posting songs she had written and recorded on MySpace. She built a following of tens of thousands of listeners on the site. She has since gone on to be hugely successful.

Word of mouth

Artists like Allen also benefit from the power of **word of mouth** (people spreading ideas) on the Internet. People use their **blogs** or social-networking pages to discuss their favorite recent entertainment finds, or they leave comments in chat rooms to spread the word. This allows everyday people to direct what becomes popular.

However, entertainment media are finding ways to take advantage of this trend.

Stealth marketing

Entertainment media are aware of the power of word of mouth on the Internet. In recent years, companies with products to sell have paid people to leave positive feedback—which is essentially advertising—in places like blogs, chat rooms, and online stores.

But this approach can backfire. For example, in 2006 video game fans became aware of a blog called "All I want for Xmas is a PSP." It seemed like a blog by a person who was desperate for the Sony PlayStation Portable (PSP), a new console. However, it was discovered that it was a fake blog Sony had created to sell its product. Many people in the video gaming community slammed Sony in real blogs and chat rooms as a result.

Spotting fake feedback

It is not always easy to spot when advertisers post "fake" reviews of their products online. However, there are some signs to look out for.

For example, it may seem odd if a product has lots of negative reviews but then one or two incredibly positive ones. In a case like this, it is possible that the company started to add positive reviews to balance out the product's overall rating. The writing in the positive reviews might seem more formal than a typical review by an everyday **consumer**, and the reviews might also make exaggerated or overly enthusiastic claims. The reviews also might not offer much evidence.

If you are uncertain whether such reviews are real, check out a variety of different websites to see what other people are saying.

Technology of the future

Technological changes are perhaps the most exciting part of the future of entertainment media. Only 20 years ago, people did not have **MP3s** or MP3 players. They did not have the Internet as we know it. They did not have cell phones or **smartphones**. Where will technology be 20 years from now?

History has shown that as technology develops, it can do more. Also devices can get smaller and smaller. Knowing this, it seems possible that technology could move in the direction of small, single devices that can perform an amazing variety of functions.

The 2002 science fiction movie *Minority Report* featured "future" technology that allowed moving hands to control items on a screen.

Already video game consoles like X-Box and PlayStation 3 are set up to play media such as music and movies, go online, and of course allow people to play video games. The future of entertainment media will possibly build from that. Tablet devices like the iPad and the Kindle are rapidly becoming a major source of all kinds of information and entertainment, from school textbooks to video games, movies, and more.

Some people also think devices that attach to people's bodies might be a trend that has not fully developed yet. Many people use earpieces and in-ear headphones to listen to music or talk on the phone. But new devices, like visors that can be used to watch movies or play games, have led to speculation that there is more future "body" technology still to be developed.

Movie technology: What's next?

In the world of movies, technology is changing all the time. The 2009 film *Avatar* used state-of-the-art **digital** 3D (three-dimensional) technology, **CGI**, and performance-capture technology, which records the movements of real human actors and turns them into CGI characters. Many experts believe this represents the future of technology in big-budget films.

Today, Microsoft's "Project Natal" seems to be making the fictional technology shown in *Minority Report* into a reality!

The next generation of video game technology

In the world of video games, Microsoft's "Project Natal" is a new controller-free gaming system. A console uses cameras to read players' movements. It then copies them on the television screen using avatars, meaning representations of the players on the computer screen. It seems likely that competing brands will develop similar products along these lines.

Convergence

A recent trend in entertainment media that seems likely to continue is called **convergence**. In convergence, different entertainment media combine forces. For example, Spider-Man's image is used in a movie, video game, comic book, ride, and toy. Movies based on video games, such as *Resident Evil*, are an example of convergence, as are video games based on movies, such as *Star Wars* games.

Successful movies like the *Star Wars* series can make lots of money by selling related products, such as toys and games.

Convergence makes good economic sense. Since creating entertainment media has become increasingly expensive, entertainment media often want to spend their money on surefire successes. By using a character or story that is already popular—for example, Spider-Man—they are more likely to have a hit.

What will it cost?

Another big question about the future is how people will pay for entertainment. Some experts think that most entertainment media available online are going to be distributed for free. That way, **piracy** is not such a problem. Advertisers will provide the money to pay for sites—and they will find new ways to get their

advertisements noticed. Plus people can pay a fee if they want more features.

Become a part of the future

Clearly, exciting new developments are just around the corner in entertainment media. Young people like you will be at the center of this entertainment media revolution. You will be able to take advantage of all the positive connections, experiences, and ideas that entertainment media can offer.

But remember to approach these media with your eyes wide open. Do not become so overwhelmed by your options that you simply accept, rather than question, all the information coming at you. Stop and ask yourself questions about why different forms of entertainment were made, what they show, what they do *not* show, and what they are trying to sell you. Also think about the larger consequences of entertainment media, such as the effects of violent content or pirating original material.

Entertainment media are all about fun, and that is how they should be. By being an informed consumer, you can be at the center of a whole new world of fun and games.

When it comes to entertainment media, always remember to be a questioning, critical consumer!

Timeline

c. 1440 German inventor Johannes Gutenberg develops the printing press. For the first time, large numbers of books and other documents can be printed and distributed.

1890s Gramophones and phonographs allow people to listen to recorded music by playing grooved discs.

Movies are developed as an entertainment **medium**.

1920s Radio stations begin to broadcast programming.

Sound is developed in movies.

1930s Color is developed in movies.

1950s Television becomes a common entertainment medium in many people's homes.

1960s Cassette tapes and cassette players allow people to listen to recorded music.

1970s Video arcades become popular; early home video game **consoles** are developed.

Personal computers become affordable enough for many people to have them in their homes.

Videocassettes and VCRs allow people to record television programming and to rent movies and other programming.

1980s Cable television greatly increases the number of channels viewers have to choose from.

CDs and CD players allow people to listen to recorded music with higher sound quality than ever before.

1990s DVDs and DVD players allow people to watch high-quality recordings on televisions and computers.

DVRs create new recording options for television.

The V-chip is added to television sets as a way for parents to block offensive programming from their family's television sets.

The Internet develops from a way for universities to exchange information into a worldwide way for people to share information and entertainment.

Digital effects greatly increase the **graphics** and user involvement in video games.

MP3 files allow people to purchase and exchange music on the Internet.

2000s Amazing new special effects like **CGI** change the way movies look.

Social-networking sites allow people to share music and to discuss entertainment media.

Piracy of entertainment media becomes increasingly common, hurting major entertainment media companies.

Video games overtake other entertainment media as the most **profitable** form of entertainment in the world.

The Amazon Kindle and other "e-readers" become a popular way for people to read books, magazines, and more on a small electronic tablet.

Blu-ray discs and Blu-ray players are introduced and further advance the quality of home entertainment.

The Nintendo Wii allows video gaming to become more interactive than ever before.

Smartphones allow people to access information and entertainment on the go in ways not previously possible.

Glossary

blog online journal

computer-generated imagery (CGI) moviemaking technology in which computers create lifelike, three-dimensional characters and backgrounds

console computer that plays video games when connected to a monitor or television screen

consumer person who buys things

controversial causing debate

convergence technique used by entertainment media companies in which a variety of different products and forms of entertainment—for example, movies, video games, and toys—are all built around a single character or theme

copyright legal ownership to a creative work such as a song, movie, or video game. The person who holds the copyright controls how the work is reproduced and receives any profits made off of the work.

desensitized when someone has lost his or her sensitivity toward actions such as violence

digital form of data storage that uses a series of ones and zeros in its coding

digital video recorder (DVR) recording device that records television programming using digital technology

focus group small group of people who are asked to give their opinions

graphic realistic and detailed

industry large area of business

market research group of studies done to figure out what people want, need, or believe

medium (plural: **media**) form of communication, such as a movie or video game

MP3 digital file that contains music

network television company that owns certain channels and controls the programming that is shown on them

passive not active; letting things happen, rather than making things happen

piracy when people illegally copy, use, share, or sell a product such as a DVD, video game, or CD

product placement advertising technique in which companies pay entertainment media to put their products in places like movies, songs, and video games

profit money earned from something

record label company that makes music recordings

smartphone cell phone that can perform many of the functions of a computer, such as Internet access

stereotype general idea about certain people, such as a race of people, that assumes everyone in the group is the same. Stereotypes are often negative.

target demographic specific audience someone selling a product wants to reach

word of mouth spreading of information among people about something

Find Out More

Books

Aksomitis, Linda. *Downloading Music*. Detroit, MI: Greenhaven, 2007.

Allman, Toney. *Media Violence*. Yankton, SD: Erickson, 2007.

Connolly, Sean. *Movies and Videos*. Mankato, MN: Smart Apple Media, 2010.

Connolly, Sean. *Television and Radio*. Mankato, MN: Smart Apple Media, 2010.

Frederick, Shane. *Gamers Unite!: The Video Game Revolution*. Mankato, MN: Compass Point, 2010.

Schwartz, Heather E. *Yourspace: Questioning New Media*. Mankato, MN: Capstone Press, 2009.

Shuster, Kate. *Is Television a Bad Influence?* Chicago, IL: Heinemann Library, 2008.

Websites

"The FTC Website on Entertainment Ratings"
www.ftc.gov/ratings/
This Federal Trade Commission website explains the different ratings systems currently in place for entertainment media.

"Media Awareness Network"
www.media-awareness.ca/english/index.cfm
This website explores a range of issues, including the use of violence and sex, representations of women, and stereotypes in entertainment media.

"Center for Media Literacy"
www.medialit.org
This website provides more information about understanding the ways various media work.

Places to visit

Museum of the Moving Image
35th Avenue at 36th Street
Astoria, New York 11106
Phone: (718) 784-4520
www.movingimage.us

The Paley Center for Media
25 West 52nd Street
New York, New York 10019
Phone: (212) 621-6600
www.paleycenter.org

Topics to research

To learn more about entertainment media, do research on the
following topics:

- Consumer pressure: How can people comment on or complain
  about entertainment media content? What are the most effective
  ways of doing so?
- Moviemaking technology: What technological developments
  have influenced movies the most? How does motion-capture
  technology work?
- Obesity and its relationship to television and video gaming
- The link between organized crime and piracy
- Women and video gaming: What do women gamers have to say
  about stereotypes in games?

Index

3D (three-dimensional) technology 47

"ad-blocking" software 33
advertising 5, 24, 33, 34–35, 40, 45, 48–49
Allen, Lily 44
arcades 8
Avatar (movie) 9, 47

blogs 45
"body" technology 47
books 12, 15
Bowling for Columbine (movie) 21

cable television 8, 33
Call of Duty video games 18
Columbine High School 20–21
commercials. See advertising.
computer-generated imagery (CGI) 9, 47
convergence 48
"copycat" crimes 22–23
"cracked" files 37
Croft, Lara 29

desensitization 19, 20, 21
Die Another Day (movie) 34
digital versatile disk (DVD) 8, 37
digital video recorders (DVRs) 8, 33

Edwards, Rob 31
Entertainment Software Rating Board 25
ethnicities 30, 31
E.T.: The Extra-Terrestrial (movie) 34

focus groups 12–13

freedom of speech 19, 23, 25

Gore, Al 18
Grand Theft Auto 4 video game 18, 28, 29

Halo 3 video game 9

In Rainbows album 41
intellectual property 39
Internet 9, 33, 37, 39, 43, 45
iPad tablet 46

Jonze, Spike 15

Keys, Alicia 29
Kindle tablet 46

Manson, Marilyn 18–19, 21
market research 12, 14, 15
Meyer, Barry M. 39
Meyer, Stephenie 12
"modding" 37
money 9, 11, 12, 13, 14, 15, 33, 34, 35, 37, 38, 39, 40, 41, 48
Moore, Michael 21
Motion Picture Association of America 25
movies 7, 8, 9, 11, 12, 13, 14, 15, 17, 18, 22, 23, 25, 29, 31, 34, 35, 37, 38, 39, 43, 46, 47, 48
MP3 files 7, 9, 13, 17
music 7, 9, 11, 13, 15, 17, 18–19, 29, 31, 34, 38, 39, 40, 41, 43, 44, 46, 47
music players 7, 9
MySpace 40, 44

Natural Born Killers (movie) 22–23

Nine Inch Nails (band) 41
Nintendo Wii game console 9, 14

organized crime 38

passive viewing 5, 35
Patel, Dev 31
peer-to-peer file sharing 37
Pinto, Freida 31
piracy 37, 38, 39, 40, 41, 48, 49
Pirate Bay website 39
PlayStation game consoles 9, 14, 45, 46
The Princess and the Frog (movie) 31
product placement 34–35
"Project Natal" gaming system 47

race 27, 30, 31
radio 7
Radiohead (band) 41
rap music 17
ratings systems 25
Reese's Pieces candy 34
reviews 45
Reznor, Trent 41
Ritchie, Guy 18
role models 29, 31
Runescape video game 40

Saving Private Ryan (movie) 17
"sex objects" 24, 28
sexual imagery 5, 24, 29
Shakira (musician) 31
Sims video games 35
Slumdog Millionaire (movie) 31
"smartphones" 5, 9
Smith, Will 31
social-networking sites 40, 44, 45
Spider-Man character 48

Spielberg, Steven 17
Star Wars series 48
stereotypes 5, 27, 28, 29, 30, 31
Stone, Oliver 22, 23
Svensson, Eva-Britt 28

Tarantino, Quentin 18
target demographics 12–13
television 5, 7, 8, 11, 12, 24, 25, 29, 33, 34, 35, 43
test audiences 13, 14, 15
timeline 50–51
Tisseron, Serge 19
Twilight (Stephenie Meyer) 9, 12

V-chip technology 25
videocassette recorders (VCRs) 8
video game consoles 5, 8–9, 14, 37, 43, 45, 46, 47
video games 5, 8–9, 11, 12, 13, 14, 17, 18, 21, 25, 28, 29, 34, 35, 37, 38, 39, 40, 43, 45, 46, 47, 48
video-sharing sites 44
violence 5, 17, 18–19, 20, 21, 22–23, 28, 49

websites 9, 33, 39, 43, 45
Where the Wild Things Are (movie) 15
women 24, 28, 29
word of mouth 45

Xbox game consoles 14

Yorke, Thom 41
YouTube 33, 44

DATE DUE